The 3P Advantage

1. Positive: The opportunity and ability to act; to fulfill one's potential.

2. Proud: Gratified; feeling honored, satisfied, or happy about a fact or event.

3. Productive: Capable of producing something, especially in abundance.

How to Develop Positive, Proud, & Productive People

For *Their* Success and
the Success of *Your* Organization

How to Develop Positive, Proud, & Productive People

The Walk the Talk Company
P.O. Box 210996
Bedford, TX 76095

Printed in the United States of America
13-digit ISBN: 978-1-885228-94-9

Credits

Copy Editor	Kathleen Green, Positively Proofed, Plano, TX info@PositivelyProofed.com
Design, art direction & production	Melissa Cabana, Back Porch Creative, Plano, TX info@BackPorchCreative.com

INTRODUCTION

If there's a "magic" formula for developing successful people (who in turn help your organization become successful), would you want to know what it is?

Hopefully your response is a resounding "Yes!" because you're holding the answer in this handbook. There's definitely a formula for success, and the good news is, it's not magic! But, it does depend on three key factors that, when combined, have maximum impact.

Let's call it the "3P Advantage" in which people are equally *positive, proud,* and *productive.* You'll soon learn why it's impossible to separate one from the others when achieving the ultimate success.

First, recall a time when you achieved personal success. It could be a long-term goal you reached, a calculated risk that you were brave enough to take, a physical achievement, or the time you spoke up when no one else would. Big or small, this moment is meaningful to you.

Think about the unique abilities you used to fulfill your potential. Perhaps the achievement caused you to stretch further than you dreamed possible. Most likely, you had to *earn* this success – nothing was handed to you. But overcoming roadblocks is part of what makes this achievement all the more **positive**.

Other people may or may not know about your success. It's nice to receive public accolades, but the real payoff is how it made you feel about yourself. Just thinking about it can make you feel happy. It was a satisfying experience that you're willing to go after again. Why? Because you felt **proud**.

These types of moments are measurable – something changed. There was a "before" and "after." You moved the needle and it felt good to see the result of your hard work. It's the kind of accomplishment that makes you say it was a good day, because you did something that mattered. You were **productive**.

Positive, proud, and productive. It's impossible to have sustainable success in just one area without the other two. Now imagine an entire organization made up of people operating with the 3P Advantage. What level of success could be reached? You don't have to guess. There are organizations already putting the 3P Advantage into action.

Every year the Great Place to Work® Institute compiles a list of the 100 best companies to work for based on certain criteria. This is more than a checklist of perks and benefits. From the employee's perspective, the best places to work are ones where there's a culture of trust, pride in one's work, and employees who enjoy working with each other. Not surprisingly, these same organizations are all high-performing. When employees feel positive and proud, they're productive.

Makes sense, right? So if this 3P formula is so great, why isn't every organization already doing it? You, along with others, may have tried. But, unless there's a proper understanding of what the three concepts mean and how to apply them, the advantage turns into a *disadvantage*. Here's a brief summary of each concept and some common misunderstandings:

What it means to be POSITIVE

Positive work cultures have optimistic leaders who are grounded in reality. Every work setting will have its challenging employees, customers, and circumstances. The difference is in how you address these things. A positive approach means highlighting exceptions to the problems by catching people doing things right and using something called solution-focused problem solving. When competencies are used to address deficits, employees are far more likely to respond in a positive way.

Being positive is:

- ✔ Realistic optimism
- ✔ Noticing what's going right
- ✔ Using solution-focused problem solving

What it's NOT:

- ✘ Absence of challenges
- ✘ Ignoring problems
- ✘ Pretending that everything and everybody is "Great!"

What it means to be PROUD

It's gratifying to know that the work you do matters. When others appreciate your contributions, you care even more. Soon your job becomes more than just a paycheck; it's a source of pride. This deep level of satisfaction needs to be earned. It's impossible to come by if bosses are micromanaging. Instead, it requires a delicate balance of setting high expectations, coaching skills, and allowing employees to mentor each other. When you can call success your own, you feel proud.

Being proud is:

- ✔ Ownership
- ✔ Accountability or self-management
- ✔ Satisfaction

What it's NOT:

- ✘ Arrogance or false pride
- ✘ Entitlement
- ✘ Maintaining the status quo

What It Means to Be PRODUCTIVE

There's great satisfaction in starting and completing a task. Most times that would be possible if it weren't for all the interruptions: meetings, technology, chatty Cathy, and bosses who pile on projects. The most productive work environments allow employees to fully dive into a project for shorter, more intense periods of time, without interruption. Great managers remove obstacles, focus efforts, and value energy (as well as time) so that employees can be highly productive.

Being productive is:

✔ Working in short, concentrated blocks of time

✔ Removing obstacles

✔ Managing energy, as well as time

What it's NOT:

✘ Working through interruptions

✘ Endless workflow with no completion

✘ Juggling multiple projects and making little or no progress

When these three concepts are humming along in harmony, people actually *enjoy* coming to work. They know they'll be treated with respect because their work matters, and they'll leave having accomplished something.

Added Bonuses

One bonus of creating this magical trifecta is that recruitment and retention become much easier. Your employees do the marketing for you by bragging about where they work. They also feel honored by becoming part of the hiring and training team. After all, they're the ones who will have to work with the new hire, so employee input is invaluable.

Another benefit of the 3P Advantage at work is that the positive effects naturally overflow into one's personal life and community. When you're spending eight hours a day being positive, proud, and productive, it's easier to practice the same success skills in the rest of your life.

So, now you know the "magic" formula! It's time to break it down into applicable tools so your staff and organization can start to experience increased success. Ready? Turn the page and let's get going!

TABLE OF CONTENTS

1. Start With a Positive Platform

Build an Optimistic Workplace

Imagine you're playing on a sports team that's getting tromped by your opponent. At halftime, with a score of 50-0, what would you want to hear from your coach?

1) "You might as well give up now because there's no way you're going to win."

2) "Remember, you guys are AWESOME! You can totally turn this around! All it takes is *believing* that you can!"

3) "We're in a tough situation. You have what it takes to score if we tighten up the game plan. Let me remind you of your strengths, what we practiced, and how to recognize opportunities."

The first coach's response is pessimistic. You know the type – the Debbie Downer, glass half empty, Eeyores of the world. They don't call themselves negative; they're just being "practical." So, whatever you do, don't get your hopes up.

It's safer to expect the worst so you won't be disappointed when it happens. This type of manager hardly inspires others to achieve their best, especially during tough times.

Coach #2 is the opposite. This person's yippee skippy, pie-in-the-sky, smiley-face enthusiasm can be just as draining. They're full of blind optimism. All they see is possibility because their blinders prevent them from acknowledging anything negative or challenging. This type of manager is confusing positive thinking with staying positive while facing very real obstacles.

Coach #3 has the safest perspective: *flexible* optimism. The level of optimism is realistically adapted to the situation, yet remains positive. Here, the coach shows belief in the team's talents and strengths to form a winning game plan. Flexible optimists don't ask whether the glass is half full or half empty. They ask where is the source of the water and how can you get more. This mindset is what forms a positive platform.

Flexible optimists don't ask whether the glass is half full or half empty. They ask where is the source of the water and how can you get more.

Cultivating a culture of optimism pays off in tangible benefits. Research suggests optimism is tied to better health, relationships, problem solving, productivity, and promotions.

The Science of Optimism

Do you have to be born optimistic or can you learn it? Optimism is a way of thinking that can be learned. Psychologist Martin Seligman, author of *Learned Optimism*, says that the difference is in how you explain events.

When a setback occurs, optimists assume it's temporary, changeable, and isolated. Pessimists explain the same event as permanent, unchangeable, and pervasive. So, if the computers break down, an optimist reacts as if the problem will be fixed soon and it won't affect the rest of the day. A pessimist says, "The *entire* day is ruined! Why do I bother showing up? This *always* happens to me."

When a positive event occurs, the reactions are opposite. An optimist assumes it's permanent and far-reaching whereas a pessimist assumes it's a fluke and can't be repeated no matter what you do.

Quick Quiz: How Optimistic Are You?

1. In general, you expect life to be:
a) easy   b) hard   c) challenging

2. Before meeting a new person, you assume:
a) we'll be best friends   b) I'll be negatively judged
c) positive regard

3. When problems arise, you think:
a) it's no big deal   b) they'll never get fixed
c) they'll get solved eventually

4. When you receive positive praise, you think:
a) everyone loves me   b) they're lying   c) I can earn it again

5. When you receive corrective feedback, you think:
a) the other person was having a bad day   b) I can't do anything right   c) I can improve

6. If you don't know an answer, you believe:
a) it doesn't matter   b) you're stupid   c) you'll figure it out

7. When others experience good fortune, you assume:
a) your lucky day is coming   b) nothing good ever happens to you   c) you're able to earn success

---

You can encourage staff to respond with flexible optimism by helping them explain events in a positive way. When either a setback or victory occurs, ask these questions:

Five Coaching Questions to Grow Optimism

1. How did you personally influence the outcome?

2. How will this benefit other areas of your work or team?

3. What can you learn from this situation to help you in the future?

4. How did the way you thought about this situation affect the outcome?

5. Review the situation and note every opportunity you had to make a decision. What decisions will you repeat next time and which ones will you change?

When people respond to these questions with self-awareness and appropriate perspective, keep encouraging flexible optimism. If they should respond with a pessimistic attitude, challenge their explanations by realistically exploring the facts. Eventually, you can train automatic responses to be more optimistic.

USE SOLUTION-FOCUSED PROBLEM SOLVING

Optimism and problem solving go hand-in-hand. Again, thinking optimistically doesn't mean you won't have problems, but it does affect the way you go about addressing them. The highest-performing teams use a method of problem solving called "solution-focused." It's built on these premises:

- Focuses on what people want to achieve versus the problem that made them seek help or complain

- Assumes every problem has exceptions

- Focuses on competencies versus deficits

- Focuses on the present and future versus the past

- Assumes change is constant

To be clear, solution-focused *doesn't* mean that you provide all the answers! Instead, you ask questions to uncover strengths and resources that guide people to their desired outcome and away from complaining.

In short, they discover their own solutions, making them feel proud of their own efforts.

Just think about how most people respond to workplace problems. Without strong leadership, it's easy to drop into complaining, negativity, and gossip. Let's take a typical workplace problem and see how you might address it using the solution-focused approach.

Solution-Focused Problem Solving in Action

Problem: An employee enters your office looking frustrated and angry. When you ask what's wrong, you hear a five-minute rant about a difficult co-worker who refuses to cooperate and is "intolerable."

Solution-focused response:

- ◆ Identify the real problem. Ask the frustrated employee what he or she wants to achieve. Better communication? A more respectful relationship? What would that look like? The real problem is not a difficult co-worker (complaining), but how to improve the relationship.

- ◆ Since every problem has exceptions (a time when the problem wasn't occurring or it wasn't as bad), ask when the working relationship was better. How can those moments be expanded?

- ◆ Focus on competencies by exploring what each person was doing when the relationship was better.

- ◆ Focus on what changes need to be made right now to reach and maintain a healthier relationship.

- ◆ Remind the employee that change is constant, therefore gains are lost if not reinforced, and difficult times are temporary.

As you can see, the circumstances remain the same, but the solution-focused response doesn't indulge complaining. Instead, it encourages a conversation about what the employee is seeking. It's the difference between saying, "This is what I need and here's my plan to achieve it" versus "Here's what's wrong and why." Clearly, the first response is much more positive.

Chronic complainers will need some coaching to help them become more solution-focused. They're in the habit of elaborating on what's wrong as if that will solve the problem. In fact, it only leads to more frustration and dead ends. You'll need to develop a different set of ears to clarify the real problem that leads them forward toward solutions.

Here's a three-step process to help complainers refocus.

Workable solutions require:

1. **Reworking the problem.** This requires encouraging employees to discuss what they need or want versus what's currently not working. For example, if an employee is feeling stressed and overwhelmed, the workable solution becomes how to feel more calm and in control.

2. **Establishing a goal.** When measurable goals are in place, the solution process moves forward. A person seeking to be calm at work might set a goal of taking a daily lunch break, asking for help on big projects, or delegating tasks. The goal is phrased in positive terms of what the employee *will* do versus *won't* do.

3. **Increasing something.** To remain positive, a workable solution must increase something, focusing on what you want more of, rather than less. In the case of a stressed employee, the person could increase effective communication, deep breathing, outside exercise, training skills, etc. So, if an employee intends to "stop working so late," that becomes "leaving the office on time five days a week."

Benefits of Being Solution-Focused

- More positive
- Encourages collaboration
- Saves time and money because solutions are reached sooner
- Can be used in multiple situations

Does the solution-focused approach work in every situation? There will always be certain circumstances where you need to know what's wrong in order to solve it. If you take your computer into the repair shop because it's making an odd noise, you will need to focus on the cause of the problem to get it fixed.

But, when it comes to people problems, such as managing staff and personal growth, more often than not, the solution-focused approach works. Even using it 50 percent of the time results in a more positive, encouraging workplace culture.

When we take time to notice the things that go right – it means we're getting a lot of little rewards throughout the day.

– MARTIN SELIGMAN, AUTHOR

2. MAKE PEOPLE PROUD TO 'CALL IT THEIR OWN'

MANAGE THE BIG PICTURE

When it comes to setting goals for your staff, what's your big picture? If you're reading this handbook, one of your big-picture goals is surely to help them feel proud of the work they accomplish. Yet, on a daily basis, many supervisors respond in ways that make people feel anything but proud because they're being micromanaged.

If you think about what makes you feel proud, it's when you've engaged in an activity that required you to work hard to achieve something. It's not so much about the end goal but the process by which you earned it.

Imagine that you wanted to run a marathon, so you hired a coach to help you train. After weeks of hard work and dedication, the big day arrives. With sore muscles and blistered feet, you finally cross the finish line with your coach cheering for you from the sidelines. Compare that with training and starting the race, but halfway through, your coach gives you a ride to the finish line. In both examples you'd reach the finish line, but only one of them would make you feel proud.

In much the same way, micromanaging steals an employee's thunder and undermines success. Yes, it can be tempting to interrupt or take over a task when an employee is struggling or moving too slowly. There might be momentary relief, but what do you really gain in the big picture? Take a look at the signs of micromanaging versus managing the big picture and assess your current approach:

Signs of Micromanaging

- ◆ Supervisor solves all problems; rarely consults others
- ◆ Supervisor interferes and "improves" others' work
- ◆ Supervisor resists delegating work
- ◆ Employees don't receive necessary training or coaching
- ◆ Employee work is closely monitored and controlled

Negative Results of Micromanaging

- ✗ Increased workload and stress for supervisor
- ✗ Repeated problems that never get resolved
- ✗ Dissatisfied and apathetic employees
- ✗ Low productivity
- ✗ Poor team morale with little trust
- ✗ High employee turnover

Signs of Managing the Big Picture

- ◆ Supervisor coaches employees to solve their own problems

- ◆ Supervisor delegates tasks that help employees learn new skills

- ◆ Supervisor encourages employee autonomy, offering feedback when necessary

- ◆ Supervisor concentrates on bigger projects while staff handles the day-to-day tasks

- ◆ Employees receive ongoing training

Positive Results of Managing the Big Picture

- ✔ Positive work environment where employees feel valued

- ✔ Increased productivity; innovative thinking

- ✔ Fewer problems persist because they get solved faster

- ✔ Confident, invested employees

- ✔ Increased trust and accountability

- ✔ Entire team grows in skills and experience

Obviously, managing the big picture earns better results for the whole team. When they do well, you benefit, too. If you recognized a bit of the micromanager in yourself, here are four ways to begin taming the impulse to control too much:

1. **Delegate.** If you're focusing on all the little stuff, the big stuff isn't getting done. Begin to delegate meaningful tasks that will help teach your staff new skills. At the same time, stay relevant by growing your own skills as you focus on bigger, more complex projects.

2. **Schedule updates.** Set up a regular (but reasonable) schedule to receive project updates. Give employees enough time to make progress or develop questions,

but not so much freedom that an irreversible error might occur.

3. **Encourage problem solving.** When problems arise, resist the urge to immediately solve them. Instead, use it as an opportunity to teach necessary skills so that employees can handle similar situations independently without relying on you.

4. **Transform concerns.** If you still feel the need to closely monitor everyone's work, ask yourself what skills or experience an employee needs for you to feel more confident. Focus on teaching those skills versus taking the task over yourself.

Your ultimate job as a leader is to grow future leaders, not assume a new position and keep doing your previous job plus everyone else's. That's not the best use of your talents or their skills.

ENCOURAGE OWNERSHIP AND PERSONAL RESPONSIBILITY

> Accountability breeds response-ability.
>
> – STEPHEN R. COVEY, AUTHOR

Remember the first car you bought with your own money? Or, maybe you inherited the family car, but something changed when it became *yours*. Chances are that your level of care and attention stepped up a notch as soon as that vehicle had your name on it.

In the same way, employees show a new level of appreciation and dedication when they own their work. A big part of that is setting clear goals that are tied to organizational goals. It takes more than just handing over the keys to the car – they have to know where to drive it.

Quick Assessment: **Ask Employees to Complete These Statements**

1. **Each day, I am personally responsible for**

    _____.

2. **My work directly impacts** _____.

3. **I contribute to the organization's success by**

    _____.

Become a goal facilitator.

Once you deliver clear, specific goals to your employees that are directly tied to the organization's big picture, now what? Your job is to become a goal facilitator. Do everything you can to break down barriers to their success and you'll see personal responsibility instantly increase. Here's how:

Turn over the process. Allow people to own the process of goal achievement whenever possible. Outline objectives, timelines, and parameters and give them the freedom to accomplish the goals. This inspires creativity and ownership.

Provide resources. Help people obtain the resources they need to get the job done, such as materials, training, labor or additional expertise.

Schedule time. Nothing is more frustrating than to be given an objective and no time to accomplish it. Find ways to help staff carve out chunks of time to work on their goals and reach a quality outcome.

Navigate politics. Every organization has its share of red tape that makes it hard to get things done. Think ahead and anticipate possible snags. Then do what you can to clear the path so your employees experience success.

Praise Positive Performance. Offer encouragement and support by using the Positive Performance Checklist.

POSITIVE PERFORMANCE CHECKLIST

Make sure the feedback you provide is:

✔ **Timely.** Don't wait. Give recognition as soon as possible after the positive performance takes place. Praise tends to lose its effectiveness with the passing of time.

✔ **Specific.** Tell people exactly what they did that was good. A mere "nice job" really doesn't say all that much. Being specific tells people what behaviors to repeat in the future.

✔ **Sincere.** Insincere praise is usually worse than none at all. Be honest and open. Tell people what their performance means to you personally.

✔ **Individual.** Focus on individuals rather than groups. The fact is, not all team members contribute equally.

✔ **Personal.** Adjust the style and method of your recognition to the receiver. Some people like public praise while others prefer private discussions. Give "different strokes to different folks." Not sure what they prefer? Ask!

✔ **Proportional.** Match the amount and intensity of recognition to the achievement. Going overboard for small stuff will make people question your motives.

The ultimate measure of our lives is not how much
time we spend on the planet, but rather how much
energy we invest in the time we have.

– JIM LOEHR AND TONY SCHWARTZ,
AUTHORS OF THE POWER OF FULL ENGAGEMENT

3. ENERGIZE OTHERS TO BE PRODUCTIVE

USE PARKINSON'S LAW TO EVERYONE'S ADVANTAGE

Have you ever experienced these circumstances?

◆ You had months to prepare for a big holiday, but crammed all your tasks into the last two weeks.

◆ You knew about a work proposal for weeks, but wrote it just days before it was due.

◆ In school, you had all semester to read a book, but waited until the last week to start it.

If these scenarios sound familiar, then you've experienced Parkinson's Law: **"Work expands to fill the time available for its completion."**

Cyril Northcote Parkinson, a British historian who spent years working for the British Civil Service, made the observation in 1955. It means that if you give yourself a week to complete a two-hour task, then the task will grow in complexity and become more daunting to fill the week. It doesn't necessarily mean more work is created, but stress and tension surrounding the task increases to fill the extra time.

This isn't to suggest that you should do everything fast and at the last second, producing shoddy work. But it's always good to assess how much time is really necessary for any given task. The most productive teams spend the right amount of time on the right things while maintaining quality and energy. *Working longer on a task doesn't automatically produce higher quality.* Many times it's just an excuse to procrastinate, which drains energy the longer you put it off.

The reality is that many tasks could be completed in less time by picking up the pace and setting shorter deadlines. When you know you have to get something done – you do it.

Think of it this way: If you had to cut an hour off of your workday – but still had the same responsibilities – how would you accomplish them? What tasks would you have to do more efficiently, adapt, or even eliminate as unimportant? What if every employee had to streamline his or her job this way? As a manager, it's your job to help employees assess the right time for a task and help cut the red tape so things can actually be accomplished.

Assessing for Time-Fillers

Done correctly, re-evaluating tasks for the real time it takes to complete them versus the inflated version results in an energized team. However, done incorrectly, employees feel pushed beyond the brink of their abilities and become overstressed under-performers. Take great care to find the right balance.

Here are some ideas on how to use Parkinson's Law to everyone's advantage:

- Experiment with completing routine tasks in half the time with a non-negotiable deadline. What happens?

- Set specific goals to be achieved by lunch or the first half of a shift. Have employees report their progress.

- Divide big jobs into smaller tasks with shorter deadlines so that employees give laser-focused attention to one small, specific goal.

- Cut the number of meetings you have and the time spent in them by half. Remain standing versus sitting.

> If you had to identify, in one word, the reason why the human race has not achieved, and never will achieve, its full potential, that word would be "meetings."
>
> — DAVE BARRY, AUTHOR, HUMOR COLUMNIST

Involve your staff in this process and engage their ideas. You may find that work tasks have been accurately assessed for time, which is great! You may also learn that a bit of time inflation has crept into the system, bogging down productivity. Here's the bonus for everyone: Getting things done feels good. If extra time is not adding to quality, cut it.

Multitasking Is a Myth

It's popular to believe that people can multitask, but research shows that the human brain can only concentrate on one mental task at a time. So, you can walk and talk at the same time (a *physical* and mental task). But, you can't talk and type at the same time and fully concentrate on both activities. The brain learns sequentially and focuses on one thing at a time. This is true for everybody, no matter your age.

In fact, the term "multitasking" is misleading. It should be "task switching" because that's really what your brain is doing. Research shows that task switching is so inefficient that it can reduce productivity by as much as 40 percent. Why?

Does Age Matter?

Interruptions reduce concentration and productivity, whether you're young or old. As we age, it can take longer to refocus on the original task due to a decline in working memory.

Because your brain has to constantly start and stop rather than continue on one track. Imagine a train moving in one direction. At every interruption, it has to stop, move to another track, start and stop again, and then switch back to the original track. The process may only take one-tenth of a second to switch tasks, but it adds up. The more complex the tasks, the more productivity drops and errors increase.

Mono-tasking: One Thing at a Time

In terms of productivity, the most efficient way to work is to mono-task – to focus and complete one thing before moving to the next task. Unfortunately, most jobs require us to "multitask." Many workers might feel insulted or would be bored if you suggested that they're only able to focus on one thing at a time, depending on the complexity of the tasks.

Survey Employees

Just about every job includes tasks and responsibilities that could be completed far more efficiently if the employee could focus without interruptions. While you can't restructure every job, with the help of your employees you can assess how and when people could carve out short blocks of time to concentrate on one major task.

Another technique is called "batching" where related tasks are grouped together instead of spread throughout a shift. For example: designating short blocks of time when emails and voicemails are answered instead of constantly checking throughout the day. When similar tasks are batched, you can accomplish a lot more in less time.

> **Personal Reflection**
>
> What task could you make significant progress on if you had a block of uninterrupted time? How would it make you feel to make measurable progress?

Minimize Interruptions

How often has someone's "quick question" eaten up 15 to 20 minutes of your time? These minor interruptions can add up to major losses. You can help increase employee productivity by setting these guidelines:

- ◆ **Establish a process for questions.** When and how should questions be addressed? Assess if it would be efficient to email or ask in person, keeping in mind that constant interruptions reduce productivity.

- ◆ **Determine what's really urgent.** There will always be some issues that need immediate attention, but certainly not every question is a crisis. Provide examples of questions that can be addressed within 8 to 24 hours versus right now.

- ◆ **Protect blocks of time.** If employees have been given a block of uninterrupted time to focus on a task, help them protect it. That might include redirecting calls and emails, changing locations, or giving permission to close an office door with a sign indicating when the person will be available. Some organizations use a flag system. When a red flag is posted near a workstation, it means they're on block time. (As long as you follow up on the work completed, this system won't be abused.)

MANAGE ENERGY, AS WELL AS TIME

It doesn't do any good to carve out time for a project if you don't have the energy to complete it. Authors Jim Loehr and Tony Schwartz state in their book, *The Power of Full Engagement,* "Energy, not time, is the fundamental currency of high performance." Are you and your team energized for peak performance? Let's start by looking at the signs of high versus low energy:

Signs of high, positive energy	Signs of low, negative energy
• Engaged • Confident • Invigorated • Challenged • Healthy personal and professional relationships	• Disconnected • Fearful • Exhausted • Bored • Isolated, defensive

Personal Reflection

On a scale of 1 to 10, (with 10 being highest), how would you rate your energy level? How does this impact your staff?

There are 24 hours in a day. As hard as you may try to squeeze in another hour, you can't change that fact. What is controllable though is how energy is used within that time limit – especially at work. You may think you have little influence on the energy levels at work, but actually there's a lot you can do. Here are five ideas:

5 Ways to Encourage Positive Workplace Energy

1. **Monitor work pace.** Every organization's workflow varies. There will be times of increased intensity and relatively slower moments. A high-paced environment can be energizing only if there are times of rest. Help employees establish a reasonable workflow rhythm that matches demands. Remember that being "crazy busy" doesn't automatically equal being highly efficient or productive.

2. **Take work breaks.** Creativity and productivity increase when regular breaks are taken outside of work. If you see employees working through breaks or eating lunch at their desk, encourage them to change their environment during breaks. (This is a great behavior for you to model.)

3. **Walk and talk.** Movement increases energy flow. Whenever you can, conduct one-on-one meetings by walking and talking. If the weather allows, take meetings outside for a brisk walk.

4. **Exercise.** If your organization provides an exercise facility or outside walking environment, help employees design their workday to include a timeout for exercise. Or, invite an outside exercise specialist to teach employees simple exercises they can do at

work like stretches, shoulder rolls, isometrics and deep breathing. They'll come back newly invigorated!

5. **Ask about hobbies.** Engage employees in regular discussions about their outside hobbies and watch for their eyes to light up. Share your passions as well. Taking an interest in what really excites people helps ignite a flame within them that flows into the workplace.

Mirror, Mirror

Did you know that positive (and negative) emotions are contagious? It's true! Our brains are wired to recognize and reflect the emotions and behaviors of the people around us with something called "mirror neurons."

This type of brain cell causes you to react similarly to performing an action versus watching someone else perform the same action. It's the reason sports fans feel the same joy of victory or agony of defeat as the actual players. Or, movie audiences cry right along with the lead actor they're watching on the screen. Or, you might watch someone recoil at the smell of rotten food and you wrinkle your nose and cover your mouth as if you had tasted it. Have you ever watched someone yawn and instantly done the same? All of these are empathic reactions because of mirror neurons.

Psychologist Shawn Achor, author of *The Happiness Advantage*, suggests a fun exercise to use in your next staff meeting to reveal the power of mirror neurons. Pair up employees and instruct one person to look at his or her partner with a straight, non-emotional face, no matter what the other person does. Instruct the other partner to look into the eyes of the non-emotional person, think pleasant thoughts, and offer a warm, sincere smile. The pair must maintain eye contact for 30 seconds.

Notice what happens. Inevitably, the straight-faced person can't help but break into a smile or even laughter. No amount of self-control can overpower the brain's mirror neurons. Use this bit of scientific research to impress upon your 3P team that everyone plays a key role in maintaining the flow of positive workplace energy. And, remember the positive influence you personally can have with each and every employee.

Building Emotional Muscle

If you've ever worked to the point of feeling burnt out, then you know how it feels to have little patience for others or tolerance for challenging circumstances. Your energy reserves have been depleted. Another way to think of it is the emotional muscles of positive energy are weak. Just like building physical muscle, emotional muscles can be exercised and strengthened.

Imagine that you hired a trainer to get you into shape. You meet in the gym on the first day, and the trainer instructs you to lift some weights. After a few reps, your arms might tire. Would the trainer allow you to quit? Most likely you'd be instructed to complete one more rep, then rest. Muscle is built in the pushing of limits, followed by rest and recovery.

Emotional muscle is built the same way. In terms of positive energy, the emotional muscles are confidence, patience, and empathy. At work, you are the trainer. It's your job to provide projects, feedback, and opportunities that challenge people, but also include times of recovery. Too much of one or the other will either lead to being overly stressed or underperforming. The right mix can strengthen positive energy, which will directly increase productivity.

Innovation Time

One way some organizations have balanced the mix is by offering "innovation time" or "20 percent time" for employees to work on their own ideas. A certain amount of time is set aside each week or month to give employees the freedom to explore new, creative endeavors. Not only can this help stave off boredom and stimulate energy, but the right idea can increase revenue and boost productivity.

It can seem risky to offer time now for innovation, but when is the right time? If there's no effort put into future planning and product development, what you're doing now will soon be obsolete. That's why creativity programs have also become a popular way to help retain employees in a competitive market.

4. TAKING YOUR TEAM TO THE NEXT LEVEL

HIRING AND TRAINING THE 3P WAY

Have you ever been part of a work team and wondered how one or more of its members got hired? Maybe there's a personality clash or someone seems allergic to hard work – whatever it is, you can't figure out how he or she earned a spot on the team. That doesn't happen when you hire and train people the 3P way.

So far you've learned how to grow your team to be **positive, proud, and productive**. Your team is in a groove and working well together. How do you add to the mix without disrupting the current culture? Using the 3P mindset, you involve your team in the process.

First, recruitment of qualified candidates automatically becomes easier using the 3P Advantage because employees naturally share the positive vibe of their work setting with friends and family. Instead of grumbling and complaining about poor conditions, your staff is talking up how great it is to be valued and to have pride in one's work. Positive word-of-mouth from insiders is the best kind of advertising!

So, when it comes to hiring, you want to involve members of your team in the process because they know exactly what it will take to succeed. Peer interviewing promotes high morale and accountability because you're involving staff from the beginning and showing that you value their opinions. Team members take it seriously because it directly affects their outcome.

> I am convinced that nothing we do is more important than hiring and developing people. At the end of the day you bet on people, not on strategies.
> — LAWRENCE BOSSIDY, FORMER COO OF GE

Peer Interviewing Process

Before involving your staff in the interviewing process, you need to have a clear system in place that identifies goals, objectives, and methods. Everyone is not a trained interviewer, so your team will need guidance. In addition, you don't want to thwart high productivity by pulling people away from their jobs for long periods of time. Here are the steps to put a plan into place:

Identify responsibilities, skills, and characteristics. Review the job description with your team and ask for their input on the most important qualifications. Based on this information, create a decision matrix with a simple rating system to ensure fairness and consistency.

Supervisor screens candidates. It's your job to present qualified applicants to your team based on the agreed-upon skills and character matrix. It's understood that the supervisor feels comfortable hiring any candidate passed on to the peer interviewing process.

Select peer interview team. Choose two to three employees who would be working closely with the new hire (without duplicating areas of expertise). For example, one person might represent customer service while another might focus on specific job skills. Limiting the number of people on the interview team minimizes loss in productivity and also doesn't overwhelm job candidates.

Prepare peer interview team. Review the interview matrix with your team and instruct each to prepare two behavioral-based interview questions to reveal desired skills (examples listed on page 42). Guide your team to focus on learning if the job candidate has the same values of being *positive, proud, and productive.* This portion of the interview is a two-way street meaning that the applicant can ask the employees questions, too. Give your team permission to be honest. Set a maximum time limit of 30 minutes so employees can remain productive.

Rate and summarize. Once the team has completed interviewing and rating each candidate using the decision matrix, a leader is chosen to analyze and share the data. If more discussion is needed, the team leader will organize a meeting. The team's decision is shared with the supervisor.

Examples of Behavioral-Based Interview Questions
The goal of any job interview is to really get to know the person and learn how he or she would perform within your

organization. The best way to do that is to ask behavioral-based questions instead of ones that allow applicants to give rehearsed answers like, "Where do you see yourself in five years?" Behavioral-based questions are ones that delve into how a person would perform in specific, job-related scenarios.

By now you've built a 3P team, so it's important that all new hires are screened with this in mind. Interview questions should reflect the values of being *positive, proud, and productive.* Here are some examples of behavioral-based questions in each area:

POSITIVE Interview Questions
"Tell me about the last time a co-worker or customer got mad at you."

"Tell me about the toughest decision you made in the last six months."

"Tell me about a time when you lacked the proper resources to complete a required job or task. What did you do?"

PROUD Interview Questions
"Tell me about a time when you knew you were right but still had to follow directions or guidelines."

"Describe the most meaningful praise you ever earned."

"Describe the biggest work-related problem you've solved."

PRODUCTIVE Interview Questions
"Tell me about the last time your workday ended before you completed all your work."

"Give an example of a work project that you found energizing."

"During a typical workday, how do you spend time on your breaks?"

These types of questions are designed to get the candidate talking rather than giving a limited or canned response. Spontaneous answers reflect a far more honest representation of the person. Use these examples or share them with your team to inspire more job-specific scenarios. Ask each interviewee the same questions for a fair comparison.

Cross-Training Your 3P Team

Athletes understand that if you only train one set of muscles, you're more prone to injury. The overworked muscles can easily become strained and the underworked muscles are too weak for recovery. The solution is cross-training – that is, working different muscle groups to increase overall fitness, lessen strain, and stave off boredom.

Workplace cross-training offers the same types of benefits. A well-designed program can help keep your 3P team healthy while reducing costs and turnover. Companies that cross-train report that employees have higher job satisfaction, morale, energy, productivity, creativity, and team work. It could also give an organization greater scheduling flexibility and may even result in operational improvements.

Perhaps, best of all, employees are teaching each other. This provides a professional growth opportunity and shows your faith in their abilities past a particular job. To successfully cross-train, you must realize there are some limitations, too. It won't be appropriate for every single job or task, especially if the job is highly specialized. In addition, some team members may not be interested in cross-training either out of low motivation or fear that they may *lose* their job if someone else can do it, too. You'll need to be clear about the benefits of participation and why it offers *more* job security rather than *less.*

6 Steps for Successful Cross-Training

1. Identify the tasks of each job that could be successfully completed by another person and that would be of value to learn.

2. Identify employees interested in cross-training. (Forcing resistant employees to participate may be counter-productive.) If cross-function awareness is key to team performance, some might start with shadowing another employee while others may choose to learn more.

3. Cross-train members of the same team to allow for someone to be able to step in and perform significant functions of another person's position.

4. Train the trainer. Employees who've been doing the same job for years may not realize how to explain it in beginner terms. You'll need to coach staff on how to train others in a clear, supportive manner.

5. Reduce the workload while cross-training. Otherwise, the task of teaching becomes burdensome and can brew resentment.

6. Recognize the employees who have learned new skills. Provide opportunities to practice them on a regular basis.

Incorporating cross-training into professional development plans and considering newly acquired skills in promotions will help increase enthusiastic participation. A strong team is like a strong body with all its muscles fully developed.

MAKING A DIFFERENCE IN WORK AND LIFE

Now that you've developed your 3P team, you'll notice there's a natural extension from work life into personal life. It's nearly impossible to be *positive, proud, and productive* for 40 hours a week without experiencing the positive benefits in the rest of your life. That's why a 3P work environment includes community service, connections, and relationships. This takes cross-training to a new level because people get to hone their professional skills in a whole new environment and context. The more your team experiences the positive impact they can have on others, the more energized they become.

There are multiple benefits to community involvement. It gives your organization an opportunity to build a positive reputation and provides employees a chance to be recognized outside of work. Potential employees are able to see the caliber of individuals you hire as they interact with those they serve, which makes recruitment easier. Meanwhile, your employees bond through supporting a common cause, which stimulates their interest and conversations, and gives renewed meaning to their work. Here are 10 ways your organization can get involved in your community.

10 Ideas for Community Involvement

1. **Enter a local race or walk.** Build team spirit by training and racing together in a local run, walk, or bike ride. Those who don't want to enter can volunteer to sponsor a water station, serving and encouraging participants.

2. **Beautify a community space.** Adopt a community garden space that employees beautify and maintain, such as the entrance to a school, library, park, or senior center. Post a permanent sign in the space thanking volunteers for their work.

3. **Host a Toastmasters club.** Toastmasters International is a nonprofit organization that teaches leadership and public speaking skills. Members meet weekly to give speeches and provide feedback to one another. Start an employees-only club or one that's open to the community. For more information, visit www.Toastmasters.org.

4. **Sponsor employee membership in a local business group.** Instead of having top management join local business clubs, sponsor team members who are being groomed for leadership. Examples of business/ service clubs include Chamber of Commerce, Lion's Club, Soroptimist, and Rotary Club.

5. **Mentor students.** Encourage employees to grow their coaching skills by mentoring high school and college students involved in DECA. This international program prepares emerging leaders and entrepreneurs for careers in marketing, finance, hospitality, and management. Learn more by visiting www.Deca.org.

6. **Speak at a school career day.** Schools often invite local businesses to participate in career day. Employees share about their education, training, typical day, and answer questions.

7. **Sponsor a community health fair.** Form an internal committee to coordinate with a local hospital or your insurance provider. Typical health fairs include

health screenings, outside vendors, and presentations on topics like stress management, exercise, and healthy cooking.

8. **Become a drop-off location.** Allow your business to be a drop-off location for annual collection drives, such as your local food bank, Toys for Tots (www.toysfortots.org), or Coats for Kids (www.coats-for-kids.org).

9. **Host a Red Cross blood drive.** Contact your local Red Cross chapter to learn how to become a host location. This is a great way to garner goodwill from inside and outside of your organization.

10. **Poll employees for their volunteer interests.** Ask employees which causes are important to them. Caring about and supporting employees in their personal interests builds loyalty far beyond job expectations.

Volunteering is good for business on many levels. Research shows that employees report feeling better about their organizations – and themselves – when they're presented with the opportunity to volunteer.

Those same employees develop a strong loyalty toward their company, are proud to work there, are satisfied with their employer, and are likely to recommend their company to a friend. And Millennials who participate in their company's volunteer program are more than twice as likely to rate their work culture as "very positive," as compared to those who don't volunteer. Sounds like a 3P team!

If you find it in your heart to care for somebody else, you will have succeeded.

– MAYA ANGELOU, AUTHOR/POET

REVIEW AND CLOSING THOUGHTS

Positive. **Proud. Productive.** Individually, each of these goals is powerful. But, woven together, they form the 3P Advantage, and that's magical! The ultimate success depends on fully understanding the meaning of these goals and then, of course, putting a plan into action.

To be **positive** means to practice flexible optimism and focus on solutions. To be **proud** means to achieve deep satisfaction from earning your successes. And, to be **productive** means to manage energy and time so that things actually get done. It's a foolproof formula when you apply it. But, nothing gets done without action. Here are the 10 most important takeaways for gaining the 3P Advantage:

1. **Employees want to be engaged.** The most positive and productive organizations create environments in which employees are appropriately challenged, encouraged, and rewarded. In return, they'll remain loyal and hardworking.

2. **Look for the exceptions.** Solutions are the things happening between the problems. By highlighting examples of when things are going right, employees learn to be solution-focused.

3. **Promote accountability.** Communicate the end goal to your employees and allow them to contribute and manage the process of achieving it. The more skin they have in the game, the more they will care.

4. **Be a goal facilitator.** Help employees achieve goals by limiting interruptions, cutting red tape, batching tasks, and streamlining the process. When you do your job, employees can do theirs.

5. **Bust the multitasking myth.** Re-design tasks to allow employees to become completely immersed for concentrated amounts of time so they can make significant progress. It's more efficient than skimming the surface of several tasks and not completing anything.

6. **Keep the energy flowing.** Encourage staff to balance intense workflow with regulated breaks. Eat lunch outside, take a walk, listen to music, or simply stretch. Maintain positive energy by finding opportunities throughout the day to revive.

7. **Recruit the right people.** If you want to have a 3P Advantage workplace, then screen for the qualities of positive, proud, and productive people. Let current employees participate in the interview process so they're invested in the outcome.

8. **Build a strong team.** Cross-train individuals and teams to stimulate thinking, teach new skills, and increase understanding between team members. It's easier to care and support someone when you know the person and the job.

9. **Make community connections.** People are proud to work for an organization that invests in their local community. Provide outreach opportunities or host community events at your workplace. Asking employees about personal causes shows that you care.

10. **Model the 3P life.** The best way to inspire others to become positive, proud, and productive is to model these qualities, both personally and professionally. Engage fully in your own passions, process, and goals. Get fit in all areas of your life: physical, mental, spiritual, financial, and relational. Live it versus talk about it, and then watch how contagious the 3P Advantage can be!

About the Author

Susan Fee is a clinical counselor, trainer, keynote speaker, coach, and human resource development professional. Known for her engaging and enlightening style, Susan helps individuals and clients dig deep to find their own source of inspiration. Her audiences span multiple industries, including health care, technology, finance, and education.

Learn more about Susan Fee's professional services and resources by visiting her website at www.**SusanFee**.com

About the Publisher

The Walk the Talk Company

Since 1977, our goal at Walk the Talk has been both simple and straightforward: to provide you and your organization with high-impact resources for your personal and professional success.

We believe in developing capable leaders, building strong communities, and helping people stay inspired and motivated to reach new levels of skills and confidence. When you purchase from us and share our resources, you not only support small business, you help us on our mission to make the world a more positive place.

Each member of the walkthetalk.com team appreciates the confidence you have placed in us, and we look forward to serving you and your organization in the future.

To learn more about us, visit **walkthetalk.com**.

How to Order this Book

How to Develop Positive, Proud, & Productive People

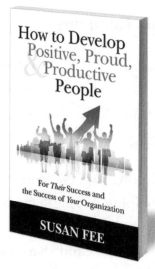

$10.95

To order additional copies of this powerful handbook,
visit **www.walkthetalk.com** or call us at 888.822.9255.
It would be our pleasure to help you
with your ordering needs.

For quantity discounts, please email us at
info@walkthetalk.com or call **888.822.9255**.

Other Recommended Management Development Resources

The Manager's Motivation Handbook – How to develop passion and positive performance with everyone on your team. *The Manager's Motivation Handbook* is a practical tool to deal with one of today's most important and yet challenging leadership responsibilities ... GETTING OTHERS MOTIVATED! **$10.95**

Listen Up, Leader! – Be the type of leader everyone will follow! This best-selling leadership book provides powerful insight into what employees want and need from their managers, supervisors, and team leaders. It pinpoints the behaviors and attributes necessary to be the kind of leader that employees will follow ... to higher levels of success. **$10.95**

212° the extra degree – This powerful resource will immediately capture the attention of everyone in your organization and motivate them to new and higher levels of performance. It will encourage anyone who reads it to give that extra degree of effort ... the extra degree that will produce exponential results! It's the message that's motivating millions! **$10.95**

To learn more about our hundreds of resources designed to help managers become more effective and respected leaders, visit **www.walkthetalk.com**

Resources for Personal and Professional Success